Ta

*methuen* | drama

LONDON · NEW YORK · OXFORD · NEW DELHI · SYDNEY

METHUEN DRAMA
Bloomsbury Publishing Plc
50 Bedford Square, London, WC1B 3DP, UK
1385 Broadway, New York, NY 10018, USA
29 Earlsfort Terrace, Dublin 2, Ireland

BLOOMSBURY, METHUEN DRAMA and the Methuen
Drama logo are trademarks of Bloomsbury Publishing Plc

First published in Great Britain 2021

Series design by Rebecca Heselton

Cover image: Wolfgang Rottmann/Unsplash

A catalogue record for this book is available from the British Library.

A catalog record for this book is available from the Library of Congress.

ISBN: PB: 978-1-3502-8063-2
ePDF: 978-1-3502-8064-9
eBook: 978-1-3502-8065-6

Series: Modern Plays

Typeset by Mark Heslington Ltd, Scarborough, North Yorkshire
Printed and bound in Great Britain

To find out more about our authors and books visit
www.bloomsbury.com and sign up for our newsletters.

## Author's introduction to Bones

The idea behind this play comes from the recent exposure
by local historian Catherine Corless of the discovery of
babies' bones and skeletons found in the grounds of a
mother and baby home in Tuam, County Galway, Ireland.
The home was built on the grounds of an old workhouse
and ran from 1921 to 1961. My play is loosely based on these
recent and historical events but is not a docu-drama of
Tuam's buried babies, though it draws inspiration from the
story. Told through the eyes of Grace and her
grandchildren, *Bones* is a play about loss, the punishment of
unmarried mothers and the legacy of demonisation of
women by Church and State, where the human and
reproductive rights of women are undermined.

Since writing this play, in October 2019 abortion was
decriminalised and became lawful in Northern Ireland.
A new framework for lawful abortion services came into
effect on 31 March 2020.

### Tanika Gupta MBE, May 2019

Please note, there will be scenes of an upsetting nature.

The author would like to acknowledge and thank the BBC
Radio 4 documentary 'The Home Babies'.

### Introduction from the Royal Central School of Speech and Drama

*Bones* is the eighth annual commission by the Royal Central
School of Speech and Drama, University of London. The
play was developed over an academic year with students
from the MA Acting (Contemporary) course. The
commissioning programme has encouraged leading female
playwrights to write ambitious large cast plays, with the
freedom to explore social, political and artistic ideas, with a
large 'canvas', that need not be immediately commercially
viable. The aim is to enable playwrights to explore material
and/or experiment in form with a large cast available for

development work. Meanwhile, the students benefit from working alongside a leading playwright from the early stages of the commissioning process through to the realisation of a final production, acting as researchers, workshop participants, readers of early drafts and ultimately the original cast. This work is supported by experienced, professional, creative and production teams.

**Martin Wylde, Royal Central School of Speech and Drama**

*Bones* was performed at the Courtyard Theatre, Royal Central School of Speech and Drama, from 24 July–27 July 2019 with the following cast and creative team.

| | |
|---|---|
| India | **Courtney Buchner** |
| Connor | **Sam Wightman** |
| Sean | **Dominic Varney** |
| Emily | **Bobbi Nunes** |
| Younger Grace | **Grace O'Brien** |
| Older Grace | **Katurah Morrish** |
| Jimmy | **Dion Lloyd** |
| Michael | **Jack Tivey** |
| Ava O'Connor/Margaret | **Polly Jordan** |
| Bridget/Deidre | **Hana Kelly** |
| Frank/Politician | **Alessandro Piavani** |
| Annie/Sharon | **Lillian Bornstein** |
| Matty | **Oliver Lyndon** |
| Billy | **Jack Harrison** |

| | |
|---|---|
| Tanika Gupta | *Writer* |
| Diane Alison-Mitchell | *Co-Director* |
| Martin Wylde | *Co-Director* |
| Sammy Dowson | *Designer* |
| Sam Waddington | *Lighting Designer* |
| Will Thompson | *Sound Designer* |
| Morwenna Rowe | *Voice and Accents* |
| Bethan Clark for RC- Annie | *Fight Direction* |
| Andy Shewan | *Production Manager* |
| Adam Burns | *Stage Manager* |
| Patricia Swales | *Deputy Stage Manager* |

# Bones

## Cast

**India**, *oldest of the cousins. 31. Woman. Photographer. (English accent.) Confident, mature and experienced in life.*
**Connor**, *oldest of the three siblings. 28. Banker. (Irish accent.) Bossy and arrogant. Bullies Sean.*
**Sean**, *youngest of the siblings. 21 year old. Student. (Irish accent.) Lacks a little confidence but decent young man.*
**Emily**, *middle sibling. 25 years old. (Irish accent.) Adores India, very cheerful.*
**Grace**, *ranges from 16 to 30 years of age. (Irish accent.)*
**Jimmy**, *Grace's older brother. 21 years of age when we see him. (Irish accent.)*
**Michael**, *Grace's boyfriend/lover. (Irish accent.)*
**Sean, Connor** *and* **Emily** *are brothers and sisters.*
**India** *is their cousin. Their dads are brothers, sons of Grace.*

*Other characters to be played by ensemble.*

*Local village youth dancers, Ava O'Connor, Bridget, Deidre, Frank, Annie, Sharon, Margaret, Politician, Matty, Billy,*

# Act One

### Scene One

*An empty small lounge in a house somewhere in County Galway, Ireland. In the background we can hear the chatter of laughter and raised voices. A party is going on. Music is playing too.*

*Four young people enter* **India**, **Connor**, **Sean** *and* **Emily**. **India** *is carrying a bottle of rum and* **Emily** *four glasses. They are subdued as they settle in an armchair, on the floor etc.* **Connor** *takes/ snatches the bottle off* **India** *and pours a little rum on the floor.*

**Emily**   Not on Gran's carpet! She'll go mad!

**Emily** *bites back her words – realising – upset.* **Connor** *pours out four equal measures. They all take a glass and raise them high.*

**India**   To granny Grace. May she run wild and free.

**All**   Granny Grace!

*They all knock back their rum and* **Connor** *immediately pours them all another.*

**Sean**   Very smooth.

**India**   Cuban rum's the best. A few of these and you want to salsa.

**Emily**   I'd love to go to Cuba.

**India**   We should plan a trip.

**Emily** (*excited*)   Really? You'd go with me?

**Connor**   Don't cream your pants, Emily. Have some dignity.

**Emily** *pulls a face at* **Connor**.

*A shout goes up in the next room.*

**India**   They all seem very cheerful, don't they? Given that it's a . . . you know . . .

**Emily**    They're celebrating her life.

**Sean**    She baked the best cakes.

**Connor**    Her bedtime stories were wild. Gave me nightmares though. Especially the ghost stories. Remember the one where she claimed to have seen the devil sitting astride a grave in the church?

**Sean**    Ohhh . . . that scared the shit out of me. Said the devil smiled at her. Never quite worked out if she really did believe she saw the devil or if she was just pulling me leg.

**Connor**    Away with the fairies she was.

**Emily**    Thought she'd go on forever. Can't believe she's . . . spoke to her that evening on the phone. She sounded tired but asked me a million questions about my course.

**India**    Always was full of questions.

**Sean**    I spoke to her last week. She was a bit rambly – didn't make much sense. Kept saying she was tired of searching.

**Connor**    Yeah – said that to me too, when I called her. Asked her, searching for what? She changed the subject. Then, just before we said goodbye she said: 'Just remember, a brave soldier never looks back'.

**Emily**    Maybe she knew.

**India**    Probably. Strange being back here again. Time warp.

**Connor**    Full of ancient people drinking to her 'good health'.

**Sean**    She'd be so pissed off she's missed the best party in her house. All her friends.

**India**    And enemies.

**Emily**    Some of them are well weird. An old fella in there kept trying to pull me into a corner saying he wanted to 'tell me stuff – in private'.

**India**    The old bald bloke? He's creepy. Did the same to me.

**Connor**    Maybe he wanted a feel of your tits.

*The others groan.*

**Connor**    What? They're all sexually repressed in this town. Gran used to say – the local priest always preached at her when she was growing up – remember? 'Sex is a sin – unless it's used for union of a man and a woman in marriage and procreation'.

**Sean**    Lectured me when I was twelve about contraception.

**India**    The priest?

**Sean**    No. Granny Grace. Said that, when I was with a girl, I should always use a condom. So embarrassing.

**Connor**    Little did she know . . .

**India**    Gonna miss her. Only one who just loved me for me. No nagging, no lecturing, no expectations – thought everything I did or said was brilliant.

**Emily**    I know what you mean.

*There is a sudden blast of music and some whooping as people are obviously dancing next door. The explosion of music and joyous dancing feels odd to the four grandchildren as they all look to the door.*

**Connor**    Are those old codgers all dancin' in there?

**Emily** *stands and heads to the door.*

**Emily**    Now this, I have to see.

**India** *follows her.*

**Emily** *and* **India** *laugh as they watch the scene unfold.*

**India**    Intense!

**Emily**    Christ. Yer da's really going for it.

**India**    Look at Great Uncle Jimmy. Never seen him dance before.

**Emily**   How old is he?

**India**   Over eighty now.

**Connor**   Miserable ole git.

**Emily**   Don't be mean. He adored Gran – do anything for her.

**Sean**   He was crying like a baby when we first got here. Kept saying 'my little sister – my little sister'.

**India**   Bless.

*Sound of thumping as people dance intensifies.*

**India**   They're pissed!

**Emily**   We should join in. (*To* **Connor** *and* **Sean**.) Come on, fellas.

**Connor**   I can't dance.

**Emily**   It's not stopping them though, is it?

*They all exit together.*


**Scene Two**

**Grace** (*16 years old*) *is kneading dough in a bakery, expertly slapping it on the board, flour etc. Her brother* **Jimmy** *is fiddling around with a radio, trying to fix it.*

**Grace**   Jimmy, come with me.

**Jimmy**   Not my scene.

**Grace**   How d'you know? You've never been.

**Jimmy**   Can't dance.

**Grace**   I'll teach you.

**Jimmy**   Right.

**Grace**   You need to learn to dance if you're going to ask Katy Cooper out.

**Jimmy**    Who said anything about . . .?

**Grace**    I've seen the way you look at her when she comes in the shop.

**Jimmy**    You should mind your own business.

**Grace**    Thing is, girls like a young man who can dance. It's very sexy.

**Jimmy**    Grace Byrne! Mam'd have your guts for garters for . . .

**Grace** *laughs at her brother.* **Jimmy** *is annoyed.*

**Jimmy**    Stop laughing at me.

**Grace**    Just trying to give you some pointers. You're too stiff and formal, Jimmy. A bit of dancing would loosen you up. Never had a girlfriend, have you?

**Jimmy**    Will you please shut up. Getting on me nerves.

**Grace** *puts the dough to one side, covers it with a cloth and cleans her hands.*

**Grace**    I know Katy's sweet on you.

**Jimmy** *looks up, interested now.*

**Grace**    She asked Maggie if you had a sweetheart. Maggie asked me.

**Jimmy** (*pleased*)    Feckin' women. Gossips the lot of you.

**Grace**    She'll be at the dance – Katy Cooper that is.

**Jimmy**    Told you. I can't dance. Especially all that new-fangled, crazy, leaping around shite they do these days.

**Grace**    Jimmy! You sound like an old man. Twenty-one years old – young – full of life and . . .

*Suddenly the radio that* **Jimmy** *has been twiddling with bursts into life and we hear a blast of Jerry Lee Lewis's 'Goodness Gracious Great Balls of Fire' or Elvis singing 'Jailhouse Rock'.*

**Grace** *screams and jumps into dancing. She is good as she does all the new moves.* **Jimmy** *watches her aghast at first and then can't help but enjoy her movements. A woman's voice calls out.*

**Mum** (*O/S*)    Grace! Grace!

**Grace** *abruptly stops dancing and* **Jimmy** *switches off the radio.*

**Mum** (*O/S*)    Finish off down there! You're needed in the shop.

**Grace** (*calls back*)    Coming, Mam!

**Grace** *is out of breath but excited.*

**Jimmy**    You dance like that and I'll be the laughing stock round here.

**Grace**    You're just jealous.

**Jimmy**    Two left feet me, when it comes to dancin'.

**Grace**    You've never tried!

**Jimmy**    Oh – go boil your head.

**Grace**    You know I can't go to the dance without you Jimmy. Mam and Dad would never . . .

**Jimmy**    I'm not taking you.

**Grace**    Please, it's a special rock 'n' roll evening. They'll be doing up the hall with coloured lights and posters. It'll look so lovely. And they're playing all the latest hits!

**Jimmy**    I hate rock 'n' roll.

**Grace**    Jimmy. Just go – for me! You know what it's like slaving for Mam and Da in that shop. Baking, serving, baking . . . my life's ended before it's even begun. Wanted to stay in school, wanted to go to college . . . just one night . . . that's all I'm asking.

**Jimmy**    You're only sixteen, Grace. I don't want the responsibility. You're so excitable – always jumpin' around and talkin' to everyone.

**Grace**    You don't like me talking to people?

**Jimmy**    No . . . just that you get carried away and suddenly everyone's your best friend. It's annoying going anywhere with you.

**Grace**    I'm an extrovert, you're an introvert. It's a fact. Just accept it.

**Jimmy**    Point is, I can't control you.

**Grace**    I'll behave myself.

**Jimmy**    And I'm the Pope.

**Grace**    I promise. And I'll introduce you to Katy.

**Jimmy**    I don't need you to introduce me to anyone. She only lives down the lane. I can walk up to her anytime I want. I don't need you interfering in my private affairs. You talk too much.

**Mum** (*O/S*)    Grace! Hurry up!

**Grace** (*calls back*)    Yes, Mam. Coming.

**Grace** *takes off her apron, folds it up and turns to leave.* **Jimmy** *feels guilty.*

**Jimmy**    Ah look. I'll think about it.

**Grace** *flings her arms around* **Jimmy***'s neck.*

**Grace**    Thank you. You're the best brother in the world.

**Jimmy**    Get off me.

**Grace** *exits, happy.* **Jimmy** *manages to tune in his radio to another channel playing Irish folk music.*

**Scene Three**

*At the local village hall, the dance is in full swing.* **Jimmy** *stands awkwardly to one side watching as couples are dancing together rock 'n' roll style.* **Grace** *watches with excitement. She tries to pull her brother onto the dance floor but he's having none of it.*

*Eventually, a young man,* **Michael**, *shyly approaches* **Grace**. *She is delighted, and they dance together.* **Jimmy** *watches disapprovingly at first but then is distracted when a young woman starts chatting to him.* **Grace** *dances, full of joy.* **Jimmy** *eventually joins in and they all dance together.*

**Scene Four**

**Connor** *and* **Sean** *are dressed in dark suits for the funeral.* (**Connor** *looks smart,* **Sean**'s *suit is a little shabby.*) **Connor** *is helping* **Sean** *with his tie.*

**Sean**    How's Alice?

**Connor**    Same as ever. Alright.

**Sean**    Haven't seen her for a while. She got on with Gran – surprised she didn't come with you.

**Connor** *is silent.*

**Sean**    You're strangling me.

**Connor**    It's your shirt collar. It's one size too small.

**Sean**    Don't do it up then.

**Connor**    It'll look shabby.

**Sean**    At least I'll be able to breathe.

**Connor**    Time to buy a new suit.

**Sean**    I don't wear suits.

**Connor**    Yer wearing one now.

**Sean**    Funerals and weddings. That's the only time I ever wear one. No point in forking out for a new one.

*Finishes knotting the tie,* **Connor** *appraises* **Sean**. **Sean** *looks uncomfortable.*

**Sean**    What?

**Connor**    Yer a mess. You're supposed to be carrying the coffin with me. Look like a poor student.

**Sean**    It's because I'm a student that I don't have cash to buy a suit. So yeah. I am poor, and I am a student.

**Connor**    I thought you lot were supposed to have pride in your appearance.

**Sean**    Our lot?

**Connor**    Poofs.

**Sean**    What century are you living in?

**Connor**    When are you going to tell everyone? Can't keep it a secret much longer.

**Sean** *ignores* **Connor** *and takes out a comb to tidy his hair.*

**Connor**    Dad's gonna go mad when he finds out.

**Sean**    Connor. Why are you such a prick?

**Connor** *slaps* **Sean** *across the face.*

**Connor**    Hey, don't call me that.

**Emily** *enters wearing a red dress.*

**Emily**    Yeah, Connor, why *are* you such a prick? Did he just smack you one?

**Sean**    He's a shite.

**Emily**    Why are you slapping Sean? Vicious bastard.

**Connor**    Jesus wept. You still haven't changed? Hearse'll be here any minute.

**Emily**    I'm ready.

**Connor**    You're going to Gran's funeral – not a night club!

**Emily**    She loved me in this dress.

**Connor**    Go and change.

**Sean**    I think you look amazing.

**India** *enters wearing a colourful outfit.*

**Connor** *groans.* **India** *looks at* **Connor**.

**India**    Old man doesn't approve? Too twenty-first century for you?

**Connor**    It's our gran's funeral, in the middle of one of the most Conservative areas of Ireland. We'll be the laughing stock with you lot.

**Emily**    But Gran wasn't conservative, was she?

**India**    Anything but. Spent her whole life railing against the local mentality. Said they were all prehistoric.

**Connor**    The state of you all. Shabby, Hippy and Whorey.

**Emily** *is upset but* **India** *laughs and points at* **Connor**.

**India**    And Toxic Masculinity? What a merry group we make.

**Connor** *is furious and storms out.*

**Connor**    You're a fucking disgrace – the lot of you. Could have made the effort for Gran, couldn't you?

**Sean** *watches his brother go sadly.*

**Sean**    It's that bank he works in.

**Emily**    It's not the bank, it's his personality.

**Sean**    Yeah – always was a bully.

**Emily**    He's definitely got worse. He was really rude to Dad this morning. Called him a fat ole bastard.

**India**    I think he's just really upset about Gran.

**Sean**    And we're not?

**Emily**    What was he saying to you, Sean, when I came in?

**Sean**    He wants me to come out.

**India**    I thought you were out?

**Emily**    Not to Dad.

**India**    But my mum and dad know.

**Sean**    Everyone knows. Just don't want to have that conversation with Dad. Not yet.

**India**    Surely that's your business – not Connor's?

**Emily**    He's always acting the maggot these days. Thankfully, he's going back to Dublin tomorrow first thing – work – and we won't have to see him 'til Christmas.

**India**    Did Gran know?

**Sean**    I think it was Gran who told me I was gay. She told me when I was fifteen. 'Sean, I've a feeling you kick with the other foot. Good on you.'

*They all laugh.*

**Emily**    How long are you staying here, India?

**India**    Until the end of the week. Promised Dad I'd help him sort out Gran's stuff. There are boxes and boxes of stuff in the attic. Letters, papers, documents . . . I don't know what.

**Sean**    We're staying too. Our dad asked us to help.

It's gonna be a bit of a major operation. Papers everywhere. Gotta work out what to chuck and what's important.

**Emily**    Why has Gran got so much paperwork?

**India**    She was obviously a hoarder. Nightmare.

Come on you two. We've got a funeral to go to.

*They exit.*


**Scene Five**

**Grace** *is lounging by a river with* **Michael**, *the young man she met at the dance.*

**Grace**    Sure, I read it in the paper.

**Michael**    One hundred pounds you say?

**Grace**    He was only nine years old.

**Michael**    And he was awarded it by the court?

**Grace**    He was beaten badly by the teacher. Broke his arm.

**Michael**    What's a nine-year-old gonna do with all that money?

**Grace**    Spend it on lollipops?

*They both laugh.*

**Michael**    If only I got a hundred pounds every time I got beaten by the priests at school. I'd be a millionaire by now.

**Grace**    Were you a naughty boy at school?

**Michael**    I was not! Well . . . no more than anyone else. But those priests liked to whack us, so they did. Talked about God all the time but they were demons with the belt. We all used to go to school with newspapers stuffed down the back of our trousers. Imagine that!

*They kiss.*

**Michael**    Why did you give up school, Grace?

**Grace**    Didn't want to. I had this idea that . . . ah no.

**Michael**    Go on now.

**Grace**    I wanted to be a history teacher or maybe a librarian. Love the smell of books – the quiet of reading, losing myself in another world, a story . . . But I don't have the qualifications now.

**Michael**    Should have stood your ground, should have finished your studies.

**Grace**    It wasn't to be.

**Michael**    I'm off to college in a few months' time.

**Grace**    Lucky you.

**Michael** *takes* **Grace**'s *hand and kisses it.*

**Michael**    Wish you were coming with me.

**Grace** *strokes* **Michael**'s *face.*

**Michael**    Maybe you could.

**Grace**    Michael!

**Michael**    We could share rooms and whilst I was at college, you could go to night school and catch up on . . .

**Grace**    And you think my parents would let me run off with you – live in sin?

**Michael** *looks forlorn.*

**Grace**    I'll be here, waiting for you.

**Michael**    Maybe we should get engaged before I leave?

**Grace**    You're going to Dublin, Michael. All sorts of new experiences are waiting for you. I'd hate to tie you down.

**Michael**    Don't you want to get engaged?

**Grace**    Of course I do but, I'm thinking of you. All those classy, smart Dublin girls wearing make-up and lipstick and talking literature and politics.

**Michael**    I don't care about them.

**Grace**    My parents don't even know about us.

**Michael**    Does your brother know?

**Grace**    He suspects but he's too busy chasing after Katy Cooper.

**Michael**    It's been six months we've been going steady. I can't imagine being this close to any other girl.

*They kiss.*

**Michael**    I love you, Grace Byrne.

**Grace**    And I love you, Michael Kelly.

**Michael**   If you married me, you'd be Grace Kelly –
my princess.

**Grace**   No offence, Michael, but I prefer my name.

**Michael**   But if you were my wife . . .

**Grace** *jumps up and pulls away laughing.*

**Grace**   I don't want to be a princess. Just a teacher or a
librarian would do. And I don't see why a wife has to take
her husband's name – like she's a piece of property.

**Michael**   That's how it works.

**Grace**   Branded like cattle.

**Michael**   That's a very extreme thing to say.

**Grace**   You think?

**Michael**   Marriage is about becoming a couple – a unit.

**Grace**   Really doesn't sound very appealing. 'A unit.' I
thought marriage was about love.

**Michael** *jumps up and tries to grab* **Grace**.

**Michael**   Ah . . . will you stop teasing me? Will you agree to
getting engaged?

**Grace**   Maybe I want to see the world before I settle down.
I've still got things I want to do – you know like visit
Manhattan or sail a boat across the Blue Nile.

**Michael** *looks downcast.*

**Grace**   Maybe we can wait awhile – at least until you come
back from college after your first year.

**Michael**   A whole year!

**Grace**   We can write to each other – I'm not going anywhere.

**Michael**   But why do you want to wait a year?

**Grace**   I'm still young and this way, I'll know that you'll still
want me.

**Michael**    I'll still want you, Grace.

*They embrace and kiss. It gets passionate. They lie down together.*


**Scene Six**

**India, Sean** and **Emily** *are sat together, surrounded by boxes of papers. They each take out papers, read them in silence and then make a pile.*

**Connor** *enters and watches them. They ignore him. He sits down.*

*Beat.*

**Connor**    Funeral went well. Amazing turn out.

**Emily**    People came from all over the place.

**Sean**    Whole load of very straight looking people came from Dublin.

**Emily**    I saw Dad talking to them for ages.

**India**    Who were they?

**Emily**    No idea.

**Sean**    Never seen our dad cry before.

**India**    They loved Gran.

**Connor**    Your speech . . . at Gran's funeral . . . very touching, Emily.

**Emily** *does not look at her brother.* **Connor** *looks guilty.*

**Connor**    Look, I'm sorry – you know about – earlier on.

**Emily** *is furious with* **Connor**.

**Emily**    You think, just because I made the choice to wear a red dress, which Gran really liked, it's okay for you to call me a 'whore'? Is that how you speak to your poor girlfriend? I feel sorry for Alice.

**Connor**    Like I said . . .

**Emily**   Fuck off back to your job.

**Connor**   Bus isn't 'til later this afternoon. Can I help in the meantime?

**India**   Sure, take a box. Any box. We're trying to work out what we have here.

**Sean** *and* **Emily** *look at* **India** *annoyed.*

**Connor** *grabs a box and starts looking through – grateful to be included. He looks bemused as he reads.*

**India**   This is incredible. So many letters.

**Sean**   What have you there?

**India**   Letters from some convent in Galway – 'Sisters of the Virgin Mary' – Reverend Mother Margaret – can't read the surname – basically they say that they reject her 'accusation'.

**Connor**   Accusation? What accusation?

**India**   It doesn't say.

**Connor**   When's it dated?

**India**   Twenty-five years ago.

**Sean**   I have letters written to Gran from all over the world. She's systematically filed them all chronologically. This one, from a woman begging her to help her find her sisters, another one from the States claiming to have been adopted from Ireland and this one saying she thinks her babies were killed.

**Connor**   Shit.

**Emily**   The Sisters of the Virgin Mary. I've heard about this place – in the news. Like the Magdalene laundries. I think.

**Connor**   Why would Gran be accusing them of anything?

**India**   All this stuff, all these letters . . . she was gathering evidence against this Sisters of the Virgin Mary Convent – what was it? A hospital?

**Connor**   Christ.

**Sean** *pulls out a map and unfolds it out.*

*The others all gather to look.*

**Emily**   A map of the town.

**Sean**   From 1925. Big circle here.

*They all peer and try to make out the wording.*

**India**   It's a building. Sisters of the Virgin Mary. A convent?

**Sean**   Huge building, next to an orchard.

**Connor**   Isn't that where the estate is? Down the road . . .

**India**   With the playground. We always wanted to go there as kids and Gran would never let us. Instead we had to walk over to the park right on the other side.

**Sean**   Jeez – I remember that.

## Scene Seven

**Matty** *(10) and* **Billy** *(8) are play boxing, dancing around each other, fists raised, taking exaggerated swipes (never hitting each other)*

**Matty**   *Float like a butterfly, sting like a bee. His hands can't hit what his eyes can't see. Now you see me, now you don't. George thinks he will, but I know he won't.*

**Billy** *puts his fists down.*

**Billy**   Who's George?

**Matty**   Big George – George Forman – you eejit. Don't you know anything, Billy?

**Billy**   He's the fella Muhammad Ali beat, *roight*?

**Matty**   Yeah – in the Rumble in the Jungle.

**Matty** *recites Muhammad Ali's poem 'Last night I had a dream . . .'*

**Matty** *jabs at* **Billy** *and accidentally punches him hard.* **Billy** *falls to the floor.*

**Billy**   Owwwww!

**Matty** *looks guilty.*

**Matty**   That didn't hurt – did it?

**Billy**   Feckin' did!

**Matty** *helps* **Billy** *up and brushes him down.* **Billy** *uses the opportunity to punch his brother back hard.* **Matty** *stumbles back and* **Billy** *looks momentarily scared.* **Matty** *then laughs as he nurses his jaw.*

**Matty**   Good left hook, Billy.

**Billy**   You deserved that.

**Matty**   I did.

**Matty** *sits down.*

**Matty**   Nice spot this. Peaceful like.

**Billy**   There's a big sign up there says 'Keep Out'. Matty, what's a 'trespasser'?

**Matty**   I dunno. But it's not us. We're kids.

**Billy**   We're not supposed to be here.

**Matty**   Mam's not going to know.

**Billy**   Somebody might see us.

**Matty**   So – feckin' – what? Too many rules. Don't go here, don't go there, stand up straight, wash your face. I'm going to go wherever I want to, whenever I want to. Can't stop me.

**Billy**   Yer always gettin' me into trouble.

**Matty**   No one asked you to follow me. It's a free country. Do what you want.

**Billy** *looks around him, afraid.*

**Billy**   Matty, don't you find this place a bit creepy, like?

**Matty**    Creepy?

**Billy**    Yeah. You ever notice – It's always chilly here. Colder like than out there on the road. Strange that, don't you think?

**Matty**    You crack me up.

**Billy** *shivers*.

**Billy**    Can we go home now?

**Matty**    You go. I'm going to stay right here. Dream my dreams.

**Billy**    Miss O'Riley's always yellin' at me – says I day dream in class.

**Matty**    That's my point. We're not even allowed to have our thoughts to ourselves.

**Billy**    Says I don't concentrate on me books.

**Matty**    Why should we concentrate on boring shite?

**Billy**    I like books – story books – like the ones Mam reads to us.

**Matty**    Yeah. Me too. School books are the pits.

**Billy**    I want to be a story teacher when I grow up.

**Matty**    No such thing.

**Billy**    There is! The English teacher – Mr Graham. Last week he told us all about this Greek fella from ancient times called Zeus. Mr Graham talks funny.

**Matty**    That's cos he's English. That's how they speak there. Posh, like they've got something stuck up their hairy arses and all they want is to have a really big shit.

**Billy** *giggles*.

**Billy**    What d'you wanna be when you grow up, Matty?

**Matty**   A boxer – like Muhammad Ali. Or a Formula One racing driver.

**Matty** *and* **Billy** *make the noises together of racing car drivers.* **Matty** *stops abruptly.*

**Matty**   Starvin'.

**Matty** *looks up.*

**Matty**   Fancy an apple?

**Billy**   We'd get in mighty big trouble. Told never to go in there.

**Matty**   What is wrong with you? Cowardy custard – that's what you are.

**Billy**   Am not.

**Matty**   Big baby.

**Billy**   Am not!

**Matty**   There's no one here and those apples are rotting. Someone's gotta eat them. We could just climb over the fence and that tree over there looks an easy climb.

Course, if you're too scared, I'll do it on my own.

**Billy**   Go on then. I'll keep watch.

**Matty** *looks unnerved.*

**Matty**   Suit yerself.


**Scene Eight**

*Sunny day outside.*

**India** *and* **Emily** *are doing Tai chi together. Their movements are slow and focused.* **Emily** *is following* **India**.

**India**
Stand with your feet together, breathe in, breathe out.
Just like a bird, your arms float down and up
Breathe in, breathe out.

Imagine the water, you float up, then down
Breath in, breathe out.

Now push – imagine a wave rolling in – push with your
hands, moving with the water.
Breathe in, breathe out.

*At the end, they both sit down on the ground.*

**Emily**    That was amazing. You do that everyday?

**India**    Ten minutes in the morning. That's all.

**Emily**    Where did you learn it?

**India**    Mum and Dad. You know they're old hippies.

**Emily** *laughs.*

**India**    They used to make us do it when we were kids.
Hated it. But I ended up doing it anyway and now – it's
a habit.

**Emily**    Good habit.

**India**    One good habit in a sea of bad ones.


**Scene Nine**

**Matty** *has climbed the tree and harvests the apples.* **Billy** *watches
him as* **Matty** *looks out, high up now.*

**Matty**    I'm the king of the castle!

**Matty** *starts to sing loudly.*

**Matty** *begins to sing Mungo Jerry's 'In the Summertime'.*

**Billy** *gives up his watch and follows his brother up the tree. He picks
an apple and eats it.*

**Billy** *joins in and they sing together joyously and loudly – two kids
enjoying themselves.* **Matty** *jumps down off the tree and as he lands,
he hears a loud hollow thud.*

**Matty**    Wow!

**Billy** (*calls down*)    What's down there?

**Matty** (*calls up*)    Come and see!

**Billy** *hesitates and then jumps down too. We hear another hollow thud. They heave up a lid and peer down into a tank.*


**Scene Ten**

*We are back outside with* **India** *and* **Emily**.

**India**    It's been nice hanging out with you, Emily. Haven't seen you for a while. Not since, you know, you came to visit.

**Emily**    You were so helpful. Thank God I had an understanding Gran in Ireland and a big cousin in London.

**India**    We were more than happy to help.

**Emily**    If it wasn't for the two of you, I'd have a two-year-old running around my feet. Probably still be living at home and I wouldn't have been able to do what I'm doing now.

**India**    The anti-abortion laws were fucking archaic here.

**Emily**    Thank God for the referendum. Had friends all over the world who came back to vote. Demonstrations . . . parties. It was an amazing moment.

**India**    So many women's lives ruined because of that stupid law.

**India**    Come visit me in London again.

**Emily**    I will. Love your flat.

**India**    You got a boyfriend – right?

**Emily**    Yeah. He's sweet.

**India**    Bring him too. I'd love to meet him.

**Emily**   Thanks. We're both training to be physios – that's how we met. Gran was desperate to meet him. I told her all about him. I was about to bring him over here – next month. I think they'd have got on so well.

**India**   What's his name?

**Emily**   Karim. He's not Irish – I mean he's Irish – but he's not white. From Sudan.

**India**   Good for you.

**Emily**   Really tall. Makes me feel like a hobbit.

**India**   Have your brothers met him?

**Emily**   Sean – yeah. Sean's cool. Not Connor. And not Mum and Dad. I don't know how they would react. Connor's got weird views.

**India**   From another century.

**Emily**   He makes these homophobic snide remarks to Sean all the time. I don't trust him. Any chance he gets, he slaps Sean. It's horrid.

**India**   I didn't know that. Does Sean hit back?

**Emily**   No. Never. Wish he would belt him one. Sean just takes it.

**India**   Connor was always quite a violent kid. Kicked me any chance he got.

**Emily**   When we were growing up, Dad always used to slap him around. Not me or Sean – just Connor. Don't know why. Most of the time Dad was a gentle fella – but there were these moments when he lost it – usually when he was drunk – and Connor would get it in the neck.

**India**   You should tell your parents about Karim.

**Emily**   I'd be so embarrassed if they turned out to be racists.

**India**    Uncle Matty's not . . .

**Emily**    You just never know, do you? It's Dublin, not London. Scratch the surface . . .

**India**    You should give them a chance. Maybe they'd surprise you. My parents on the other hand are utterly predictable. Every time I introduce them to my boyfriends, they're really disappointed if they're white.

*They both laugh.*

**Emily**    Is there anyone special?

**India**    There might be. Early days but I don't want to jinx it. Funny, isn't it? Gran was so full of curiosity for the world. Wherever I went, she made me send her postcards and then she'd look everything up in her atlas, phone me and tell me interesting facts that I didn't even know.

**Emily**    Why didn't she leave this old town?

**India**    I remember our dads trying to persuade her to come and live in Dublin when Grandad died.

**Emily**    Totally refused. Wasn't as if she particularly liked the people here. Always calling them bigots and slagging them off.

**India**    Was it to do with the campaign – the Sisters of the Virgin Mary?

**Emily**    But she didn't need to be here to do her research. Could have done it anywhere.

**India**    Clearly, she had her secrets.

**Sean** *and* **Connor** *approach.*

**Emily**    You still here?

**Connor**    How can I go back to work? This is a head fuck! Like discovering your sweet ole gran was a spy for the Irish Secret Service.

**Sean** *pulls out a dusty old cassette.*

**Sean**    Found this in one of the boxes. Haven't seen one of those in years. Our dad used to have a player in the old Ford Fiesta.

**Emily**    I remember that ole thing. His awful mix tapes.

**Sean** *turns the cassette in his hand.*

**Sean**    Just says: Interview with Ava O'Connor.

**India**    Must be a cassette player in the house somewhere.


### Scene Eleven

**Grace** *enters, older now,* **Billy** *and* **Matty** *lead her.* **Grace** *looks around her with distaste and a little fear. She shivers.*

**Grace**    So cold. How many times have I told you boys not to play here? It's not safe.

**Billy**    We was hungry. Mam. Just wanted some apples.

**Grace**    The orchard is out of bounds. Big sign up there saying 'Keep Out'. Or have you both forgotten how to read?

**Matty**    There was no one here.

**Grace**    Give me strength. And then you went ferreting around, digging things up?

**Matty**    We just took a peek and found the thing.

**Grace** *produces a small skull from her bag.*

**Grace**    Matty, Billy – You know what this is?

**Billy** *and* **Matty** *look guilty.*

**Billy**    It's an old toy

**Matty**    A shrunken head like the Red Indians use to have.

**Grace**    It's not a shrunken head. It's a skull.

**Matty**    I know! I thought I could use it for Halloween.

**Grace**   It's a human skull.

**Billy**   How do you know?

**Grace**   This is a child's skull – and these teeth here are still intact. No wisdom teeth, so – it's probably from a child your age, Matty.

**Billy**   A real one?

**Grace**   From a dead body.

**Billy** *and* **Matty**   Eweee!

**Grace**   Where did you find this?

**Billy** *and* **Matty** *look horrified.*

**Matty**   I jumped down and fell on something hollow, echoey and I pulled it open. The thing . . .

**Grace**   Skull.

**Matty**   . . . was just lying there, so I picked it up.

**Billy**   There were loads of them. I didn't want to touch them.

**Grace**   Show me exactly where.

*The boys hesitate.*

**Grace**   Show me!

**Matty** *leads the way.*

**Grace** *climbs down and eventually ends up standing in the septic tank. She shines a torch around her. At first, she can't make out what she can see – just bundles of old cloth. And then she sees. And we see. Babies' skulls and bones are littered around the place.*

**Scene Twelve**

**Ava** *enters and makes tea. She is an older Irish woman. Nervous and dressed in an old-fashioned way.* **Grace** *enters and sits down. She places her cassette recorder on the table.* **Grace** *switches on the recorder.*

**Grace**  Now, Ava. I'm going to record this. Are you sure you're okay with that?

**Ava**  God will be my witness. If I am to be punished, it will be in the hereafter.

**Grace**  No one's going to punish you for telling the truth, Ava.

**Ava**  It *is* the truth. Tea?

**Grace**  Thank you.

**Ava** *pours tea with a shaky hand.*

**Ava**  What exactly do you want me to say?

**Grace**  I'll ask you questions.

**Ava**  And this contraption will record the conversation?

**Grace**  Yes.

**Ava**  Modern technology. Shall I be combing my hair?

**Grace**  It's not a camera, so we won't be able to see you.

**Ava** *takes out a comb and carefully combs her hair.*

**Ava**  Must look my best.

**Grace** *stirs some sugar into her tea and takes a sip as* **Ava** *combs her hair.*

**Grace**  Right. Shall we start?

**Ava**  Indeed. Oh! Biscuits.

**Ava** *gets up slowly and fetches a tin of biscuits which she places on the table and then sits down again.*

**Ava**  Custard creams. My favourite. Go on now. Have one.

**Grace**  Later – thank you. Ready? When did you start working at the Sisters of the Virgin Mary?

**Ava**  I was employed as a domestic.

**Grace**   How old were you?

**Ava**   I don't remember exactly. Ten, maybe eleven years old. It was before the war. I was an orphan and the local priest sent me there to help the Sisters. He told me that they would look after me. I thought, at the time, that he was very kind. He had a soft voice and clear eyes.

**Grace**   You didn't have any brothers or sisters?

**Ava**   A younger brother. Sean. I don't know what happened to him. The priest took him – somewhere.

**Grace**   And why are you speaking to me now, after all these years?

**Ava**   I want to leave a . . . statement . . . be a witness to what I saw, because no one is talking about it. They've forgotten.

**Grace**   Who's forgotten?

**Ava**   The world. And as the years go by, I feel . . . I feel . . . what happened in that place was a crime against humanity . . . against decency . . .

**Grace**   Ava, whilst you were there, what did you see? Can you tell me?

**Ava**   Girls coming in, at the dead of the night. Pregnant girls, sometimes as young as twelve, crying, begging to see their parents. They'd stay there throughout their pregnancy. Babies were born and then the mothers would leave. They didn't want to abandon their babies, but they had no choice. The Sisters had no feeling for the pregnant women. Saw them as sinners.

**Grace**   Were you given the job of looking after the babies?

**Ava**   No. I cleaned and gardened. We grew our own vegetables. It was hard work. The Sisters looked after the babies.

**Ava** *stops as she remembers.*

**Ava**    It was a lonely old hole. They used to crucify them.

**Grace**    The babies?

**Ava**    Yes. It was Bedlam. No books, no toys, no love, no care, just cruelty. The children's brains didn't grow. They used to rock themselves to sleep and all the time, they'd cry, or you'd hear a low-pitched whine like this.

*She makes a whining sound.*

God in heaven above, it was like hell. It was a horrid place for children. Mattresses were always wet from all the bed wetting.

**Grace**    The children were neglected?

**Ava**    And beaten. They used to beat the living daylights out of them. There was a little two-year-old once. I saw one of the Sisters get angry with her for crying and she hit her and hit her again and again until there was blood. Then she dragged the child away. Never saw her again.

**Grace**    She beat her to death?

**Ava**    I think so.

**Grace**    Were all the Sisters like this?

**Ava**    Sister Priscilla wasn't. She was the essence of kindness. She secretly taught me how to read and write whilst we did the gardening. And she gave me books to read. Sister Gabriel was always praying, Mother Anne wouldn't see a hole in a ladder but Sister Martha . . .

**Ava** *falls silent.*

**Grace**    What about Sister Martha?

**Ava**    She was the antichrist. Always kicking the children. She kicked me once and I fractured my leg when I fell.

**Grace**    Why did she kick you?

**Ava**    Because I tried to stop her hitting a little boy. He'd wet his pants. He was just a wee thing. Wasn't his fault. I felt sorry for him.

**Grace**    If you knew what you saw was wrong, why didn't you say anything?

**Ava**    How could I? Who would listen to me?

**Grace**    Someone might have.

**Ava**    I was totally cut off from the outside world and Sister Martha told me that trouble makers were sent to the local mental asylum. She was always threatening me with that. Said I was stupid and simple, and I belonged in a mad house.

**Grace**    You could have left the place, walked out.

**Ava**    I should have. But I didn't know anything about the outside world. Been there since I was a child. Where would I go?

**Grace**    You never asked any of the people who came in to help you? There must have been doctors, priests? The odd workman?

**Ava**    I was afraid I wouldn't be believed. I was seen as simple.

**Grace**    Sister Martha told you that. Why did you believe her?

**Ava**    When someone tells you every day that you're stupid and a dullard, you begin to believe it. I was like those babies. My brain never grew. And there was something else . . .

**Ava** *falls silent again.*

**Grace**    What, Ava?

**Ava**    I beg the Lord's forgiveness. I was made to do it.

**Grace**    What did you do?

**Ava**    The children and babies died like flies. They were emaciated, pot-bellied, delicate. Only the strong survived.

They were the ones who were adopted. But many others that died. I was the one who had to take their little broken bodies, wrap them and put them in the tank. That chamber of horrors – that's what I called it.

**Grace** *is quiet.*

**Ava**    I am as guilty as those nuns.

**Grace**    How many, Ava?

**Ava**    I always said a prayer over them. I wished them well on their journeys and prayed for their eternal happiness now they were free. In that dark place, I often wished the Lord would strike me down and take me with the babies.

**Grace**    How many?

**Ava** *thinks.*

**Ava**    I didn't bury them all. There were more down there before I got there. The place smelt rotten. I always cried when I was in that place. You could feel their souls. I felt like the Angel of Death.

**Grace**    How many?

**Ava**    Hundreds.

**Grace**    Two . . . three?

**Ava**    Several.

**Grace** *is stunned.*

**Ava**    I still dream about Sean.

**Grace**    Sean?

**Ava**    My brother. Always wonder what happened to him.

**Grace**    Do you remember any of the mothers that passed through there?

**Ava**    I do. Most of them were nice girls. I pitied them – especially the young ones – almost children themselves. They were all given false names by the Sisters.

**Grace**   Were you allowed to talk to them?

**Ava**   We were all controlled. We were not there to be sociable. It was a terrible place. You know.

**Grace**   Pardon?

**Ava**   I remember you. The Sisters called you Claire.

**Grace** *reaches over and switches off the recorder.*


## Scene Thirteen

**Matty** *and* **Billy** *now men and fathers are sitting with* **India**, **Emily**, **Connor** *and* **Sean**. **Matty** *is tense, whilst* **Billy** *is easy going.*

**Billy**   When we were kids, we discovered an old septic tank with a baby's skull in it. Mum went to take a look herself and discovered hundreds of babys' skeletons, wrapped in blankets in there.

**Connor**   Hundreds?

**Billy**   Yep. Hundreds. She got obsessed with finding out who those skeletons belonged to.

**Matty**   Discarded, unwanted, bastards.

**India**   What?

**Billy**   No contraception, no abortion, just blame and shame. Back in the day – even now – sometimes so-called illegitimate children were looked down on – not seen as equal to other kids. Treated like dirt.

**Matty**   To the extent that they were just left to die.

**Emily**   In this mother and baby home.

**Billy**   It used to be a workhouse and then the Sisters of the Virgin Mary took it over in the 1930s. Pregnant women went there, had their babies and then left them in the care of these nuns. The home was for the fallen, the misfortunate – the unmarried mothers had to repent for their sins.

**Emily**    Medieval.

**Billy**    The nuns arranged adoptions. That was the deal. But according to Mum's records – for a period of thirty-five years – a baby died there every two weeks.

**Connor** *quickly calculates in his head.*

**Connor**    That's – 910 babies.

**Billy**    Mostly between the ages of 0 and 3.

**Emily**    I keep finding these notes in Gran's handwriting – 'Who were these babies? How did they die? Where are their death certificates? Where are the burial records?'

**Matty**    She was bloody obsessed.

**Billy**    The home closed down in the 1970s and then they built the estate, covered up the site and built a playground on top of it.

**India**    Repulsive. A children's playground!

**Billy**    Mum's was a voice in the dark. No one wanted to listen to what she had to say. They said she was a trouble maker, trying to bring down the good name of the Church and the Sisters.

**Connor**    And you knew nothing about it?

**Matty** *and* **Billy** *exchange glances.*

**Matty**    Still have nightmares about that place. Standing – skulls and bones crunching under my feet. How you'd imagine hell. Sometimes I think I'm walking all over her dead body.

**Emily**    Whose body, Dad?

**Matty** *falls silent.*

**Billy**    Keep telling you to go and talk to someone, Matty.

**Matty**    Who am I going to talk to? It happened years and years ago.

**India**    PTSD.

**Emily** *looks something up on her phone.*

**Matty**    Eh?

**India**    Post traumatic stress disorder.

**Billy**    There are counsellors, Matty.

**Matty**    Counselling? Give me a break.

**Emily** *reads out her phone research.*

**Emily**    'Someone with PTSD often relives the traumatic event through nightmares and flashbacks, and may experience feelings of isolation, irritability and guilt.' Sounds like you, Dad.

**Matty**    Rubbish.

**Sean**    What I don't get is why would Gran keep it a secret?

**Matty**    Didn't want people knowing her business.

**Sean**    What about Grandad? He must have known. Gentle fella –

**Matty**    That he was. And he adored Mum.

**Billy**    He supported her go back to school – she got her learning, became a teacher, then a head teacher. Clever woman. I remember her telling us that her parents didn't think she should get an education because she was a woman.

**Matty**    That's how it was in those days.

**Billy**    Mum went to the local church, the Guardaí, the Government and people kept fobbing her off. Said it was famine victims from way back.

**Matty**    Unbaptized babies – condemned to hover between heaven and hell – caught in limbo.

**Emily**    Why would they all be buried so neatly in one place?

**Billy**    Exactly.

**India**   There's something you're not telling us, Uncle Matty.

**Matty**   Some things should be kept private. It's not right that we stick our noses where they're not wanted.

**Billy**   That's the problem though isn't it, Matty? People *should* have stuck their noses in.

**Matty**   Don't start.

**Billy**   Everyone turned a blind eye. They knew what went on in that Home but because of all that shite about sin and religious bollocks doctrine – those nuns literally got away with murder for decades.

**Matty**   Mum didn't want people to know.

**Connor**   What? Didn't want people to know what?

**Matty** (*snaps*)   Leave it, Connor!

**Connor**   You've asked us to go through her papers, we uncover a nightmare and you won't talk to us about what . . .

**Matty** *jumps up and shouts aggressively in* **Connor**'*s face.*

**Matty** (*shouts*)   I said – leave it!

**Matty** *exits abruptly and angrily.* **Connor** *looks upset.*

**Billy** *watches him go sadly.*

**Billy**   Sorry, Connor. He shouldn't have done that. Next time, you punch him back – hard.

## Scene Fourteen

**Grace** *is kneading dough again in the kitchen. Flour everywhere. She concentrates hard. Her mother* **Bridget** *enters and takes her coat and hat off.*

**Bridget**   Foul weather!

**Grace**   Still raining?

**Bridget**   Hasn't stopped all day. Shaunassie Street has flooded again. Shop floors awash with filthy water.

**Grace**   Poor Donna. Her shop always gets damaged by the rains.

**Bridget**   Lucky we're a bit further up the hill. You alright? Looking a bit pale?

**Grace**   I'm fine.

**Bridget** *approaches* **Grace** *and looks at her.*

**Bridget**   Definitely looking a bit under the weather.

**Bridget** *kisses her on the forehead and feels her temperature.*

**Bridget**   A little clammy. Coming down with something maybe? Such a hard worker, Grace. Maybe you should finish this batch off and then put your feet up for a bit. Got some good news, Grace. Your brother's got himself a job.

**Grace**   A real job, is it?

**Bridget**   Car mechanic at Donnagan's.

**Grace**   He's gonna get paid?

**Bridget**   He is. All that tinkering he's done over the years – finally paying off. Be good to get an extra income for the family. As long as he doesn't spend it all on the drink and that Katy Cooper. What do you think of Katy?

**Grace**   I like her.

**Bridget**   I find her voice irritating, bit too high pitched, but she seems nice enough.

**Grace**   It's great Jimmy has got a job. Be good for his self-confidence.

**Bridget**   Let's hope he keeps it.

**Grace**   He's always liked fixing things. But what does he know about cars?

**Bridget**   Donnegan thinks he's 'got the gift' and says he'll train him up. I was going to make something special tonight for dinner to celebrate. Our first born has finally got himself a half decent job!

**Grace** *smiles as* **Bridget** *whirls her around in a celebratory twirl.* **Grace** *is dizzy.*

**Bridget**   You really aren't yourself. You sure you're okay?

**Grace** *wipes her hands on her apron and braces herself.*

**Grace**   I got some news of my own mam.

**Bridget**   You're not going back to school. You know we can't afford it. We need you in the shop.

**Grace**   It's not that.

**Bridget**   That's a relief.

**Grace**   I went to the doctor's today, been feeling a bit unwell, not right. Apparently, I'm . . . I'm . . . expecting a baby.

**Bridget** *looks aghast.*

**Grace**   I'm four months gone.

**Bridget**   Are you sure?

**Grace**   Doctor confirmed it today. I heard the heartbeat.

**Bridget**'s *face contorts.*

**Grace**   Mam? You're gonna be a grandmother around Christmas probably. I know it's not ideal but Michael . . .

**Bridget**   Michael?

**Grace**   Michael Kelly – he says he's gonna marry me. So, it's alright isn't it?

**Bridget**   You think Michael Kelly's parents are going to let their precious son marry a baker's daughter, a common prostitute?

**Grace**    I'm not a prostitute . . .

**Bridget** *is furious.*

**Bridget**    You're nothing but a dirty, filthy whore. To think that my daughter would open her legs and fornicate with the first man that came her way. It's a sin against God. A terrible sin!

**Grace**    Mam. I love him.

**Bridget**    And you think he loves you enough to go against his high and mighty family to marry a loose common slut like you? A strumpet? A Jezebel? You bring shame on us all. What is your father going to say?

**Bridget** *paces in fury.* **Grace** *watches her, shocked at her mother's reaction.*

**Grace**    I want to have this baby. It was made from love.

**Bridget** *slaps* **Grace** *hard.*

**Bridget**    Shut your filthy mouth!

**Grace** *is shocked by her mother's reaction and starts to cry.*

**Bridget**    Go upstairs and pack a bag.

**Grace**    Why?

**Bridget**    Just do as your told.

**Bridget** *puts her coat back on.*

**Grace**    Where are you going, Mam?

**Bridget**    As usual, it's left to me to sort this mess out. Don't want an ugly bastard grandchild. I don't even want to look at your face. Go upstairs. Pack your bag. To think, I was so proud of my beautiful, innocent daughter. And this is how you repay me? What will people say? The shame of it! The disgrace!

**Grace**    A baby is a good thing. A beautiful new life. I don't understand why you're . . .

**Bridget**   It would have been better news if you'd told me you had cancer and were going to die. Now get out. I'm going to get the priest.

**Grace** *turns and exits,* **Bridget** *is left on her own for a moment, upset and furious, before she also exits.*


**Scene Fifteen**

**Michael** *steps forward and reads out a letter. He looks very upset.*

**Michael**    Third of August 1959

My darling Grace,

My father won't let me marry you. He has threatened to kill me if I do. He says I would be ruining my future. I don't agree with him. I love you, Grace. I would love our baby too. Please forgive me for abandoning you. I don't know what else to do. My whole family seem to be hell bent on stopping us from being together. It's like I'm under guard all the time. They keep telling me that we committed a terrible sin. But it never felt sinful when we were together. More like blessed.

They're sending me to Dublin tomorrow and I will go to college there as planned.

I will never forget you, Grace. I hope the Sisters will look after you and the baby well. Give the baby a kiss from their father. I am so sorry, Grace. Forgive me. Stay strong and when you are free, come and find me. I will be waiting for you. I'll still be wanting you.

Yours forever,

Michael

**Sean** *steps forward.* **Michael** *gives him the letter and exits.* **Sean** *stands and reads the letter.*

## Scene Sixteen

*Mother and Baby Home – 1959.*

*Sound of beautiful choral singing of nuns in the background.*

*A very pregnant* **Grace** *enters with a heavy bucket of water and a cloth. She puts the bucket down and starts to scrub the floor. In the background she can hear the whine of children crying. It is constant and relentless.* **Grace** *stops scrubbing for a moment and tries to block the sound out. Upset and fearful she feels her own bump.*

*An authoritative voice calls offstage.*

**Sister**   Claire! Who said you could take a break? Get on with it.

**Grace** *quickly gets on with scrubbing.*

*More pregnant women join her, each with a bucket and a cloth, each of them scrubbing, cleaning on their hands and knees.*

*The sounds of the whining, crying children gets louder and drowns out the nuns singing.*

## Act Two

### Scene One

**India** *is sitting with* **Frank** *(elderly) and* **Annie** *(his grand-daughter) in the garden.*

**Frank** (*American*)  We were so sorry to hear of your grandmother's death. She was such a wonderful lady.

**India**  Thank you, Frank.

**Frank**  Can't believe we missed her funeral by a day.

**Annie** (*American*)  We met Grace last summer when we first came to Ireland. She helped Gramps a lot.

**Frank**  You're the oldest grandchild, aren't you? The photographer?

**India**  Erm – yes.

**Frank**  She was so proud of you. Showed us your book.

**India**  I actually had no idea that Gran was involved in this campaign.

**Frank**  She wasn't involved. It was *hers*. She was the one who reached out to us. We happen to be here because we were going to meet her again.

**Annie**  So sad we missed her funeral. Got here for our meeting and . . .

**Frank**  She was a firecracker of a lady.

**India**  Please, do tell me how Gran was able to help you?

**Frank**  I was trying to trace my parents – at least my birth mother. I was born here – down the road in the Mother and Baby Home in 1950. I was adopted by an Irish couple when I was seven years old. They moved to the States and took me with them.

**Annie**   It was a financial transaction between the Sisters and Frank's parents.

**India**   You mean they paid money to adopt you?

**Frank**   Don't get me wrong. My parents wanted me, but they had to pay a lot of money. Years later, I discovered, I had no birth certificate, no adoption papers. It was a hell of a job getting a passport when I became adult. My granddaughter here happened to read an article on the internet that Grace had written about the Home – reaching out to anyone who had connections there.

**Annie**   I'm a pro choice campaigner myself in Michigan and I kind've stumbled across her article.

**India**   She wrote an article?

**Annie**   She posted a lot of articles. Had a website called 'The Home Babies'.

**Frank**   You didn't know?

**India**   None of us knew anything. We're just beginning to see the enormity of her work. We only discovered in the last twenty-four hours that Gran had a baby there.

**Annie**   Oh – wow – no wonder you look so shocked.

**India**   We don't understand why she didn't tell us. Was she ashamed of her past?

*Beat.*

**Frank**   I don't think it was shame. I know she thought very highly of you all and this was her mission. To highlight the wrongs of the Sisters, the Church and the State and to bring justice to all the mothers and children that went through those doors. She didn't want to burden you with an ugly past. She wanted to leave you with a hopeful future, a clean legacy.

**India**   Frank, do you remember your time in the Home?

**Frank**    Some things – yes. I remember being cold, hungry and afraid. Concrete and cement everywhere. We used to lick the moss on the walls to get some nourishment.

**India**    I just can't believe the inhumanity of those nuns.

**Frank**    They saw the women and children in that Home as subhuman.

**Annie**    Your grandmother explained to us that in those days, the priest was the centre of Irish society and that there was more fear of the priest than of the police.

**Frank**    Religion took over everything. Are you religious? I'm not offending you, am I?

**India**    God – No! I'm just finding it hard to get my head around it all.

**Frank**    The priests saw themselves as superior to everyone else – the moral guardians of society and they passed judgement on unmarried women who got pregnant.

**India**    Gran hated the old priests.

**Frank**    And as far as the Church was concerned, with their vows on celibacy, who could bring down a priest? A woman! So, they had to be carefully monitored, controlled and punished. The nuns were following orders from above.

**India**    What else do you remember about the Home?

**Frank**    We had our own secret language which no one could understand, except us kids . . . Every couple of weeks, all of us sitting around in a circle, quietly, as couples came and chose one of us to be adopted. We were desperate to be adopted – to get out of that godforsaken place. When my parents came, I remember looking up and giving the woman, who would eventually become my dearest mother, the biggest smile I could manage. I smiled until my cheeks ached. She told me that it was my smile that won her over.

**Annie** and **Frank** *laugh.*

**Annie**   And Gramps been smiling ever since.

**India**   How did you know to smile?

**Frank**   There was a very lovely Sister at the Home called Sister Priscilla. She told me – I remember, very clearly – she said 'Now Frank, when the adults come around looking for a son to adopt – you give them a great big smile. Win 'em over'.

**India**   Sister Priscilla. Her name's come up a few times.

**Frank**   They weren't all bad. Some were indifferent. But the bad ones were monsters. And then Grace told me about the bones found . . . made me feel sick to my stomach. I could have been one of those . . . poor, poor creatures. Maybe I knew some of them.

**Annie**   Gramps discovered who his mother was.

**India**   You met her?

**Frank**   I found my birth mother eventually – in the graveyard – but still – I found her. No. Sadly, I was too late. She died over a decade ago.

**India**   I'm so sorry.

**Frank**   But, with Grace's help, I did track down and meet my three sisters.

**Annie**   Looked just like him.

**India**   How was that?

**Frank**   Wonderful. They were warm and friendly. Told me so much about my birth mother. Her name was Maureen.

**Frank** *chokes up.*

**Annie**   And his sisters knew about Frank. She told them that she had had a baby in 1950 in the Mother and Baby Home. She named him Patrick and she was apparently just fourteen years old when she fell pregnant with him.

**Frank**   The nuns told my mother that I had died, so all her life, Maureen assumed that I didn't exist. She never knew I was alive and well in the USA.

**India**   Why would they lie?

**Frank**   Grace thought that there was an illegal adoption racket going on. Children like me were a saleable item. She found a birth certificate in my name – Patrick Walsh and then she found a death certificate in the archives in my name but no burial certificate.

**India**   They falsified documents?

**Frank**   Unmarked graves, illegal adoptions going back over decades. Irish babies and children were basically trafficked for money.

**Annie**   There should be a criminal investigation. Goodness knows how many Irish children were adopted in this way – without their mothers knowing! There were so many mother and baby homes in Ireland. I reckon thousands and thousands of Irish babies were illegally adopted out. The Church made a lot of money out of it.

**India**   It's . . . it's . . .

**Annie**   I know. Mind blowing.

**India**   But what about the bones in the septic tank . . . the death certificates my gran collected – 796 of them!

**Frank**   I'm sure there are babies' bodies there – and maybe we'll never know exactly who they are, or whether the death certificates tally with how many bodies are in there. Grace wanted the bones to be exhumed.

**Annie**   She always said, if you have bones, you have DNA. We have the technology to identify those remains. Put names to those babies in there. That's partly why I came over with Gramps. I wanted to interview Grace – get her story out there. She had so much information and was hitting a brick wall as far as the authorities were concerned.

*Beat.*

**India**    I could help you.

**Annie**    I was hoping you'd say that.

**Frank**    I'm one of the lucky ones. And it doesn't make me
feel so good.

**Annie**    You're a survivor, Gramps.

**Annie** *kisses* **Frank** *gently on the cheek.* **India** *is touched.*

**Frank**    I've had a good life. My adoptive parents were the
best. Loving, kind, always thought of me as their own. I met
this beautiful woman here, we had our own children and
now six grandchildren. But those first few years of my life left
me with terrible nightmares. I guess they're frightened
memories. I'm always hiding somewhere, in a shed, or
behind a wall and I can hear a woman screaming and beating
something. In my nightmare, I'm absolutely terrified.

**Annie**    He must have witnessed something horrific.

**Frank**    I went to look at the site where I was born. Place
gave me the creeps. Everyone knew about it at the time. No
one said anything. We were nicknamed 'The Home Babies'.
We wore hobnail boots. We went to school. We were made to
sit separately from the other school kids.

**Annie**    We got on so well with Grace. We love Ireland and
the people. We were just coming as friends. Such a pity we
missed her. She was one of a kind. And so humble. I don't
think she realised how important she was. She opened the
door to the authorities, so we could access the adoption files,
she gave us a voice and all those who have lived in shame
feel like a burden has been lifted.

**Frank**    Despite everything, though, I'm very proud to
be Irish.

**India**    It is beautiful here.

**Frank**    A driving holiday. A visit to my sisters but no more digging up the past. Not for me anyway. I'll leave that to you youngsters now. Not much of a legacy is it?

**Frank** *looks away, emotional.*

It's beyond words.


### Scene Two

**Grace** *is cuddling a baby. She is singing a tune. Another young, heavily pregnant woman,* **Deidre***, is with her and they coo over the baby.*

**Grace**    Isn't she beautiful?

**Deidre**    Absolutely gorgeous. And she smells so sweet.

**Grace**    I'm going to call her Keira.

**Deidre**    Lovely name.

**Grace** (*to the baby*)    Hello, Keira Byrne. Take a good long look at your mammy's face.

**Deidre**    Her eyes are open.

**Grace**    She's lookin' at me.

**Deidre**    Such a beautiful face.

**Grace**    You think?

**Deidre**    Looks like you.

**Grace**    When you grow up, you're going to be so pretty. And clever! She looks very intelligent – don't you think, Deidre?

**Deidre**    Cleverer than us, that's for sure.

*The baby cries a little.*

**Grace**    Ahhh . . . hush now.

**Grace** *rocks the baby, kisses her face.*

**Jimmy** *enters sheepish and uncomfortable.*

**Grace**  Jimmy! Look! Keira! Keira, here's your Uncle Jimmy.

**Jimmy** *looks at the baby and strokes her head.*

**Jimmy**  May you have a long and happy life, little Keira.

**Grace**  Isn't she just perfect? Look at her wee fingers and all that black hair. Beautiful.

**Jimmy**  I've come to take you home, Grace.

**Grace**  We're going home, Keira! You'll meet your grandparents and all your . . .

**Jimmy**  No, Grace.

**Grace**  What d'you mean?

**Jimmy**  You know you can't bring her home.

**Grace**  I can't leave her here.

**Jimmy**  You have to. That baby's a sin. And no one knows you're here. Mam told everyone you were with an aunt in Galway. You can't come back with the baby.

**Grace** *looks distraught.*

**Grace**  I can hide her in my room. No one will know.

**Jimmy**  Don't be daft.

**Grace**  She's mine. Please. Only I know how to look after her.

**Jimmy**  Give the baby to the girl, or I'll have to call the Sisters.

**Deidre**  I'll look after her, Grace.

**Grace** *starts to sob and clings to the baby harder.*

**Grace**  No, no, no . . .

**Jimmy** *tries to take the baby off* **Grace** *but* **Grace** *won't let her go.*

**Grace**    She's my baby girl!

**Jimmy**    Stop making such a fuss!

**Grace**    You're my brother. How can you be so hard?

**Jimmy**    This is your fault. This is the consequences of your behaviour. I warned you. I told you – you always went too far.

**Deidre**    Claire. You knew this day would come. Go and live your life. Give her to me.

**Grace**    I can't.

**Deidre**    Go. The Sisters have already found a lovely couple to adopt her. She'll grow up strong and clever and have a wonderful life.

**Grace**    You're just saying that.

**Deidre**    It's true. What can we offer our babies in this terrible place? We'd be spat at in the street, our babies would be called bastards – at least this way, they'll have a chance. You have to let go, for the sake of Keira.

**Deidre** *takes the baby off* **Grace** *who breaks down sobbing*.

**Deidre**    I'll look after her.

**Grace** *kisses the baby*. **Jimmy** *takes* **Grace** *and leads her away*.

**Deidre**    Just remember, a brave soldier never looks back.


**Scene Three**

*Music is blaring out as* **Emily** *is sorting through records with* **Sean** *and* **India**.

**Sean**    Elvis, Chuck Berry, Little Richard, she's even got Marvin Gaye and Buddy Holly.

**Emily**    What was that song?

**Sean** *flips the record off and plays 'Everyday' by Buddy Holly*.

**India**   I've heard this one. Gran used to play it all the time.

**Emily**   Yeah – Me too! She loved this one.

**India**   There's unfinished work here.

**Sean**   You thinking of taking it on?

**India**   Gran wanted the Government to organise an excavation, exhumation and identification of those bones.

**Emily**   Dad thinks it's wrong.

**Sean**   That doesn't mean he's right.

**India**   Annie works for the *New York Times*. She said she wants to write an article about Gran's work.

**Sean**   Great idea! Get some publicity going.

**Connor** *enters and the atmosphere changes.*

**Connor**   Don't think you should do that.

**Emily**   Why not?

**India**   There's enough evidence.

**Connor**   Been talking to Dad. He's worried that we're digging around too much.

**Sean**   He asked us to look at the boxes and sort them.

**Connor**   He thinks Gran wanted to keep it secret. That she was ashamed.

**Sean**   That doesn't make sense.

**India**   She wasn't ashamed.

**Connor**   Then how come she never told us anything?

**Emily**   Weird to think we've got an aunt out there somewhere.

**Sean**   Gran must have been trying to find her daughter. Makes sense, that last conversation I had on the phone with her. 'I'm tired of searching.' Kept saying that again and again.

**Emily**   So sad she never found her daughter.

**India**   Explains why she stayed in this town. Maybe she wanted to make it easier for her daughter to find her, if she ever came looking.

**Connor**   She might be one of those baby skeletons in that nasty septic tank.

**Sean** *and* **Emily** *are quiet, upset.* **India** *looks annoyed.*

**Connor**   What? I'm only stating the obvious.

**Sean** *goes back to sifting through the records.*

**Connor**   It's not up to you to suddenly blow this up and tell the world.

**India**   Maybe Gran did feel some sort of shame for what happened, but she's gone now, and we can do something good with her research. We can show the world . . .

**Connor** (*sneers*)   Show the world . . .

**India**   . . . The way women have been treated throughout history.

**Emily**   India's right. This is important. We need to stop women like Gran feeling ashamed. It wasn't their fault. They were victims!

**India**   Abortion is still, to this day, illegal in Northern Ireland. Women are still objectified, patronised, raped, not to mention the hidden cases of domestic violence . . .

**Emily**   What about the States where they're trying to turn the clocks back? Alabama? And now other more states are trying to pass these things they call 'heartbeat' bills that ban abortions after a foetal heartbeat can be detected.

**Connor**   Jeez, here we go. Fecking feminists.

**India**   Fuck you!

**Sean**   Yeah. Shut up, Connor.

**Connor** What about the victims. You think they want their privacy to be invaded by busybodies like you? Maybe those mothers don't want everyone to know their secret? Ever thought of that?

**India** That's a great argument to keep us all silenced. Let sleeping dogs lie, don't rock the boat? That's how the patriarchy thrives.

**Connor** You three – thick as thieves. Always make me out to be some kind of a . . .

**Sean** Insensitive bastard? Is that the word you're looking for?

**Connor** Gran probably realised that those fucking nuns had murdered her baby, which is why she spent her whole life trying to expose them.

**India** No shit, Sherlock.

**Emily** You really are a prick.

**Connor** What have I said now?

**Emily** and **Sean** *ignore* **Connor**. **India** *turns away*.

**Connor** Ahh – great – gang up on me, won't you. Always making me out to be the villain – just like Alice. You don't know what it's like to lose a child. You have no idea.

**Emily** *looks at* **Connor** *surprised*.

**Emily** And you do?

**Connor** *is pacing, angry and upset*.

**Sean** Calm down, Connor.

**Connor** Don't tell me to calm down! You're all against me. All of you. I see you rolling your eyes, exchanging those looks. You all hate me.

**Sean** You're being completely paranoid.

**Connor** I know. I fucking know.

**Emily** *and* **Sean** *watch their brother anxiously.* **India** *looks alarmed.*

**Emily**   You're frightening me now, Connor.

**Connor**   . . . Fucking bitch . . . took an injunction out on me. Can you believe that? Not even allowed to see my son . . . went to court . . . Told lies about me. They believed her and now . . . kid has another dad . . . I'm shoved out in the cold.

**Sean**   Wait. You telling us you have a child?

**Connor**   One year old . . . boy.

**Emily**   From Alice?

**Connor**   Got pregnant, had the baby. Beautiful boy. Jonathan – Jonte.

**Sean** *is shocked.*

**Sean**   Why didn't you tell us?

**Emily**   I'm an auntie?

**Connor**   Can't see him though. I'm banned.

**India**   What did you do?

**Connor**   Nothing. Said I was violent . . . took pictures of bruises . . . went to the police. I never fucking touched her. All lies!

**Emily**   Do Mum and Dad know? Do they know you have a kid?

**Connor**   No . . . better not fucking tell them. Or else.

**Sean**   Or else what?

**Connor** *looks lost. He starts to cry.*

**Sean** *and* **Emily** *approach* **Connor.** *They both hold him.* **Connor** *sobs and sobs.*

**India** *turns away.*

**Scene Four**

**Grace** *is sitting, quietly reading a book.* **Jimmy** *approaches and sits next to her. She ignores him.*

**Jimmy**   What you reading?

**Grace** *looks at him incredulous.*

**Jimmy**   What?

**Grace**   Since when have you ever cared what I'm reading?

**Jimmy**   Don't be like that.

**Grace** *goes back to reading her book.*

**Jimmy**   Heard you crying in your room last night. Same every night for the past week.

**Grace**   Why d'you think I'm crying, Jimmy?

**Jimmy**   And you haven't talked to me since you came home.

**Grace**   Just leave me alone, Jimmy.

**Jimmy**   You used to be full of life, full of chat and laughter. It's like a ghost came back from that place.

**Grace** *looks away*

**Jimmy**   Can't you forget her? Let bygones be bygones? Be my sister again? You know it hurts so bad, you not talking to me. We used to be close.

**Grace**   I don't have any feeling for you. You should have helped me.

**Jimmy**   What did you expect me to do?

**Grace**   You should have stood up for me. You made me leave my baby behind with those fecking witches. They're not Sisters of God. They're cold-blooded devils. And you had no feeling for my baby girl. How could you, Jimmy? How could you expect me to love you the same way as before? I look at you and I don't see the brother I looked up to. All I see is a stupid, ignorant, spineless brute.

**Jimmy** *looks upset.*

**Jimmy**    I was just doing what the parents and Father Patrick told me to do.

**Grace**    That's pathetic. Can't you think for yourself?

**Jimmy**    I was scared. They were all so angry and I thought they might kill you.

**Grace**    You could have helped me and baby Keira escape.

**Jimmy**    Where to?

**Grace**    I don't know. I could have gone to Dublin – or taken a boat to England – I could have got away.

**Jimmy**    I didn't think of that. I don't have any money to give you.

**Grace**    I can't stop seeing her face, smelling her skin. My milk's still spurting out of me. It hurts. I should be feeding her. How could they rip her away from me? I could have looked after her. She was mine.

**Jimmy**    Can you forgive me?

**Grace**    I can promise you this, Jimmy. I will never forgive you for the part you played in this. Never.

*Beat.*

**Jimmy**    I'm leaving town, Grace. Going to England – try and find work there. Can't face Mam anymore. Not after . . .

**Jimmy** *pulls a small package from his pocket and hands it over.*

**Grace**    What's this?

**Jimmy**    Letters to you from Michael. I hid them for you. He wrote when you were in the Home and then after too.

**Jimmy** *gets up and kisses* **Grace** *tenderly on the top of her head. She flinches.*

**Jimmy** *exits.* **Grace** *takes the bundle of letters, shocked and surprised.*

**Scene Five**

*We are in a café in Dublin.* **India** *is drinking coffee and reading.* **Emily** *and* **Sean** *enter and hug her. They are all dressed smartly.*

**Sean**    Hey, that article Annie wrote went fucking viral!

**Emily**    Made them all sit up.

**India**    It was Gran really. Annie said she just rearranged her words.

**Emily**    But it worked!

**India**    It definitely worked.

**Sean**    Shamed the Irish Church and State into action.

**Emily**    How've you been?

**India**    Great. You?

**Sean**    Fine.

**Emily**    End of term exams. But I've finished now.

**Sean**    She's a fully qualified physiotherapist now.

**India**    Congratulations!

**Sean**    Big day today. If only Gran was here. She'd be so made up.

**Emily**    You never know, she might be smiling down on us!

**Sean**    Wouldn't put it past her.

**India**    Is Connor coming?

**Emily**    He is.

**India**    Good. How is he?

**Emily**    You'll see for yourself.

**India**   You all still talking to each other?

**Emily**   Just about.

**Sean**   I finally sat down and had a frank discussion with Dad – about me.

**India**   How did that go?

**Sean**   He didn't send me to Reading Gaol.

**India**   But . . .?

**Sean**   According to him, he always knew. Wasn't exactly ecstatic but said it was my life and I should live it the way I wanted to.

**Emily**   That's big of him.

**Sean**   He spoke in such a small voice, I wasn't convinced – but then he suddenly gave me this big bear hug. Didn't say another word and left the room.

**India** *hugs* **Sean**.

**Sean**   Now all we need is for Emily to introduce her boyfriend to the family – then we'll have no more secrets.

**Emily**   All in good time.

*They laugh.*

**Emily**   Great Uncle Jimmy made a big fuss saying he wanted to come too.

**India**   Oh my God.

**Emily**   Phoned last week, literally begging Dad to bring him along.

**India**   Is he coming?

**Sean**   It's gonna be on the telly so Great Uncle Jimmy's going to watch it in the pub, with his mates.

**Emily**   Apparently, he's very emotional.

**Connor** *enters. He seems different – less uptight. He hugs everyone and sits down.*

**Connor**    Good to see you all. It's been months.

**India**    You look well, Connor.

**Connor**    I'm better than I was. Look, I'm sorry . . . the things I said . . . back then . . .

**India**    It was a weird time.

**Connor**    But I behaved like a total shite. Been in therapy.

**India**    Is it helping?

**Connor**    Early days – but yeah.

**India**    And your dad?

**Connor**    Thinks there's nothing wrong with him and refuses to talk to a 'shrink'. Your dad – Uncle Billy – talked to me though.

**India**    He said he was going to call you.

**Connor**    We've had a few nice chats. Told me about the day they found those babies' remains. He said that Dad actually fell. The ground gave way underneath him and he fell quite deep down. Your dad was still up at the top – but my dad ended up surrounded by all those bones. He was terrified. Screaming and trying to scrabble his way out of the hole.

**Sean**    Jeez.

**Emily**    No wonder he still has nightmares.

**India**    Weird that neither of our dads talked to us about it.

**Sean**    Protecting Gran, I guess.

**Connor**    India, when you were going through the death certificates, did you come across our aunt Keira's?

**India**    Gran found her birth certificate, but no death certificate.

**Connor**    So, she might actually still be alive somewhere?

**India**    Who knows? She might be alive and never knew that she was adopted or even who her real mother was. Or she might be one of those poor babies buried in the tank.

**Emily**    And Gran searched for her all her life.

**Sean**    But the truth will come out now.

**Connor**    Or at least some part of it.


### Scene Six

**India**, **Sean**, **Connor** and **Emily** *sit on one side of the stage as the* **Politician** *enters. He nods and smiles at them before speaking.* **Deidre**, **Grace**, **Sharon** and **Margaret** *also step forward.*

**Politician**    We give thanks to the memory of Grace Byrne who died a year ago. After decades of research and campaign work, of fighting for justice, we are grateful for her dogged pursuit of the truth.

**Grace**    I want these children to be remembered. They deserve it.

**Sharon**    We women were like insects. I sometimes thought 'My God . . . am I human or what?' I felt like I had no worth – no value.

**Grace**    I collected 796 death certificates of infants from the Sisters of the Virgin Mary. But there were no burial records. What happened to these babies? Were they killed? Or were they sold into illegal adoption?

**Margaret**    I was at the Home. I think my baby is buried in that septic tank. They were supposed to keep our children safe. But those nuns. They didn't care about them. They saw them as children of shame.

**Grace**    I know what I saw. All little bundles rolled in cloth. They were all over the place.

**Politician**   The site will be excavated in a bid to recover the remains. Forensic tests will be carried out to identify each child before 'respectful' reburials. It is only by taking the right actions now can we truly demonstrate our compassion and commitment to work towards justice, truth and healing for what happened in our past and, most especially, for those who were previously abandoned. I hope the Church will make reparation for its part in this shameful chapter.

**Sharon**   I had no sense of self in that place. It was an infernal machine.

**Deidre**   Not one day went by when I didn't think of my child.

**Sharon**   Not one day went by when I didn't think of my child.

**Grace**   Not one day went by when I didn't think of my child. I collected 796 death certificates of infants from the Sisters of the Virgin Mary. But there was no death record of my baby.

**Politician**   Those infants died of neglect, of starvation, pneumonia, curable diseases and broken bodies from punishments inflicted by the Sisters in the name of God.

**Margaret**   As far as women are concerned, we've taken a long time to come out of the dark ages in this country.

**Grace**   The Sisters of the Virgin Mary home isn't the only home in the country. The last mother and baby home only closed in 1996. An estimated 30,000 women and children went through those homes and 6,000 babies died. But I think this is the tip of the ice berg.

**Sharon**   There's a sense of loss – worse than grief. You never get over it.

**Politician**   In burying those infants in a tank in the grounds of the Home, we also buried our compassion, our mercy and we buried our humanity. No nuns broke in to our homes to take our children – we gave them up because of our morbid and perverse relationship with respectability.

**Margaret**   I tried to run away twice before my baby was born and twice – they found me. There was this organisation called the 'Crusade of Rescue' – an Irish Catholic organisation which had the blessing of local authorities to track down and bring back 'fallen women' to their native soil. They kidnapped me and forced me to stay until my baby was born. I was a prisoner in that Home.

**Sharon**   Adopting babies out was a profitable business for the Church.

**Margaret**   I want to stand those priests and nuns in a room, look them straight in the eye and ask them – what gave them the right to take away my child and sell him?

**Grace**   I've met numerous mothers who lost their babies. The sense of loss is so deep, you can barely put it into words. We have never recovered from it.

**Deidre**   Two worlds existed side by side. We were invisible because apparently, our sin was obvious to all who saw us.

**Grace**   There are unmarked burial grounds all over Ireland through the ages, going back hundreds of years. These are called 'Cillín'. These are common burial sites for those whose status or manner of death excluded them from normal Christian burial, for example, that they hadn't been baptised. Such was the grip of religion, we couldn't even bury our dead with respect.

**Sharon**   We were considered to be lesser people in society.

**Deidre**   When my son was eighteen, he came to look for me – and we were reunited. We're in touch regularly and I've tried to push the regret to one side.

**Politician**   In Varadkar's words, for a while indeed, it felt like the women in Ireland had the amazing capacity to self-impregnate and for their trouble we took their babies and we gifted them. Or sold them or we trafficked them or we starved them, or we denied them to the point of their disappearance from our hearts and from the sight of our country and in the case of the Mother and Baby Home, from life itself. Yes, we're all shocked now. We are indebted to Grace Byrne, for her persistence. Without her and her work, it would never have come to light.

Taken in conjunction with the repeal of the eighth amendment and Grace Byrne's extraordinary research and struggle, we believe that the women of Ireland are finally going towards a brighter future where their rights are upheld and where we, as a nation value them and their choices.

*Everyone exits, leaving* **Grace** *on her own.*

**Grace**    Religion was the root of everything. You got pregnant out of wedlock, you disappeared, your children vanished into thin air. If you didn't abide by their rules, you were punished. The sin of having sex outside marriage was all encompassing. The progeny of such sex were the devil's spawn. My God is up in the fields, in the air, in the trees, the garden, the animals, the children. I don't see God in a church or in any pomp and ceremony. I just talk to the air – say help me please.

**Grace** *exits.*


### Scene Seven

**Grace** *is kneading dough back in her kitchen. She is young again but more careworn.* **Michael** *enters. He is well dressed and slightly older.* **Grace** *freezes when she sees him.*

**Michael**    Grace?

**Grace** *ignores him. She is upset as she continues to work.*

**Michael**    How are you?

**Grace** *is silent.*

**Michael**   I know you're angry, but I wanted to see you. I never stopped thinking about you.

**Grace** *is silent.*

**Michael**   Where's the baby, Grace? What was it? A boy? A girl?

**Grace** *is silent.*

**Michael**   I wanted to be there for you, but I was a coward. I know that now. I should have . . .

**Grace**   What do you want, Michael? Because I'm busy right now.

**Michael**   I wanted to apologise, to see if we can . . .

**Michael** *gathers his courage and steps closer.*

**Grace**   Don't come any closer.

**Michael**   Where's the baby? You never answered any of my letters. I just want to know you're alright.

**Grace**   What do you care?

**Michael**   Of course I care.

**Grace**   How many more babies have you got littered around Ireland?

**Michael**   That's unfair, Grace. How can you say such frightful thing? Did you read any of my letters?

**Grace**   I read them, but you were too late.

**Michael**   Please don't say that.

**Grace**   You have a nerve coming here after all this time.

**Michael**   Listen to me.

**Grace**   You and I have nothing left to say to each other.

**Michael**   Grace, give me a chance.

**Grace**   You had your chance. I was young, I was a fool to think you'd stand by me. All of you. My family, your family, you all taught me a good lesson in life, didn't you? I literally fell from grace and I was abandoned and punished. But why did they have to punish my baby girl? She was an innocent.

**Michael**   The baby was a girl?

**Grace**   I named her Keira and they wouldn't let me bring her home with me. The Sisters adopted her out. I don't know where. I don't even know what her name is now or what her family are. She could be anywhere in the world.

**Michael** *looks upset.*

**Grace**   What did you think would happen?

**Michael**   I thought they'd let you keep her. It's a mighty cruel thing you've been through.

**Grace**   Do you know what that Home is like? Loveless. Cold. No compassion or laughter. Full of vindictive 'Sisters' and young girls like me having babies. First two months, I was sharing a room with a thirteen-year-old girl who cried every night. No one ever stopped to ask who the men were that got us in trouble. Why weren't you punished along with us? You lot all waltzed off to your colleges and your jobs whilst we were abused and made to do hard labour.

**Michael**   No one would tell me anything about it. I tried to speak to your parents – your dad punched me – kicked me down the street.

**Grace**   My heart bleeds for you. I could to tear your face off.

**Michael**   You've changed.

**Grace**   That I have.

**Michael**   You're grieving.

**Grace**   I've put it behind me.

**Michael**   Have you now?

**Grace**   I don't have any choice in the matter.

**Michael**   Do you still love me?

**Grace** *looks astonished at the question.*

**Michael**   I still love you.

**Grace**   All that's long gone for me, Michael. The world has turned.

**Michael** *comes closer to* **Grace**.

**Grace**   Don't.

**Michael**   We could get married now. My Da died last week.

**Grace**   I know and I wasn't sorry to hear that. He was a shite.

**Michael**   That's true. My mam said I should come and find you and marry you. That we should be together, and we should look for Keira.

**Grace** *looks moved.*

**Michael**   We can't just put it behind us – I know. But we can't let them win. I want to be with you for the rest of my life and I will try and make it up to you every day.

**Grace** *turns her face away.*

**Grace**   You're too late.

**Michael**   You deserve better than this place. You should go back to school and finish your education. I can support you to do that.

**Grace** *looks at* **Michael** *for the first time.*

**Michael**   I'm so sorry, Grace. I should have stood up to my da. He was a bully, he beat me, he beat my mam. We were both afraid of him. I was scared he'd come after you too. I thought you'd be safe in that Home.

**Grace**    I'm dead inside.

**Michael**    Jimmy told me.

**Grace**    Jimmy?

**Michael**    He came to Dublin to see me. Told me everything.

Though he lied and said you had the baby. Probably thought it'd give me incentive like, to get in touch.

**Grace**    I haven't seen him in two years.

**Michael**    He looked full of shame and sorrow.

**Grace**    It's not right, the part he played.

**Michael**    Please, Grace, let's try. We could start a family together.

You don't have to change your surname.

I just want you.

**Michael** *approaches* **Grace** *and holds her.* **Grace** *doesn't resist. Instead, she rests her head on his shoulder.*

**Michael**    We can make a good life together and we'll find our baby girl and bring her home.

*End.*

## Bloomsbury Methuen Drama Modern Plays
*include work by*

Bola Agbaje
Edward Albee
Davey Anderson
Jean Anouilh
John Arden
Peter Barnes
Sebastian Barry
Alistair Beaton
Brendan Behan
Edward Bond
William Boyd
Bertolt Brecht
Howard Brenton
Amelia Bullmore
Anthony Burgess
Leo Butler
Jim Cartwright
Lolita Chakrabarti
Caryl Churchill
Lucinda Coxon
Curious Directive
Nick Darke
Shelagh Delaney
Ishy Din
Claire Dowie
David Edgar
David Eldridge
Dario Fo
Michael Frayn
John Godber
Paul Godfrey
James Graham
David Greig
John Guare
Mark Haddon
Peter Handke
David Harrower
Jonathan Harvey
Iain Heggie

Robert Holman
Caroline Horton
Terry Johnson
Sarah Kane
Barrie Keeffe
Doug Lucie
Anders Lustgarten
David Mamet
Patrick Marber
Martin McDonagh
Arthur Miller
D. C. Moore
Tom Murphy
Phyllis Nagy
Anthony Neilson
Peter Nichols
Joe Orton
Joe Penhall
Luigi Pirandello
Stephen Poliakoff
Lucy Prebble
Peter Quilter
Mark Ravenhill
Philip Ridley
Willy Russell
Jean-Paul Sartre
Sam Shepard
Martin Sherman
Wole Soyinka
Simon Stephens
Peter Straughan
Kate Tempest
Theatre Workshop
Judy Upton
Timberlake Wertenbaker
Roy Williams
Snoo Wilson
Frances Ya-Chu Cowhig
Benjamin Zephaniah

For a complete listing of Bloomsbury
Methuen Drama titles, visit:
**www.bloomsbury.com/drama**

Follow us on Twitter and keep up to date
with our news and publications
**@MethuenDrama**